Sewing with Just One Yard

Quick, Beginner-Friendly Projects for Home, Fashion, and Gifts

Floral V. Seth

Copyright © 2025 Floral V. Seth All rights reserved. No part of this book may be reproduced, distributed, or transmitted in any form or by any means, including photocopying, recording, or other electronic or mechanical methods, without the prior written permission of the publisher,

Table of Content

Introduction
　Welcome and Purpose of the Book

Chapter One
　Getting Started with One-Yard Sewing

Chapter Two
　One-Yard Sewing Tips and Tricks

Chapter Three
　Home Décor Projects (One Yard)

Chapter Four
　Fashion & Accessories Projects

Chapter Five
　Gift & Personal Projects

Chapter Six
　Kids & Fun Projects

Chapter Seven
　Seasonal & Holiday Projects

Chapter Eight
　Beyond One Yard

Conclusion

Introduction

Welcome and Purpose of the Book

Sewing doesn't have to be overwhelming or expensive. You don't need a room full of fabric or years of practice to create something beautiful. With just one yard of fabric, you can make stylish, practical, and thoughtful projects in no time.

This book is designed for beginners and busy crafters who want to enjoy the creative process without the stress of complicated patterns or large fabric requirements. Inside, you'll find step-by-step instructions for projects you can finish in an afternoon items for your home, fashion accessories, handmade gifts, and even seasonal decorations.

Why One-Yard Projects Are Perfect for Beginners and Busy Crafters

One yard of fabric is a sweet spot for creativity. It's enough to make something substantial, but small enough to keep things simple. For beginners, this means you don't need to worry about handling huge pieces of fabric or making mistakes that waste a lot of material. For busy people, one-yard projects are quick, satisfying, and easy to fit into your day.

These projects are also forgiving. If you're still learning how to cut straight lines or sew even seams, a small project is much less intimidating than tackling a large quilt or full garment.

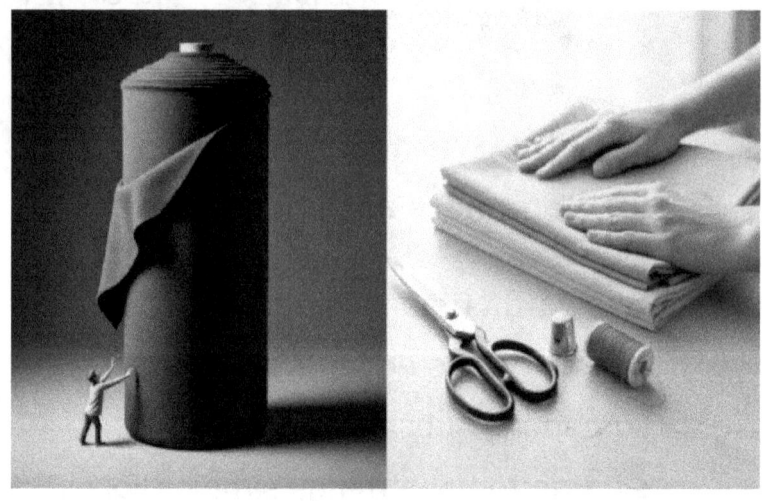

Benefits: Budget-Friendly, Fast, and Less Intimidating

- **Budget-Friendly:** A single yard of fabric is affordable and widely available. You don't need to spend much to start sewing, and many projects can be made from leftover fabric you already have.
- **Fast:** Most one-yard projects can be finished in an afternoon or even during a coffee break. This makes them perfect for building confidence and getting quick results.
- **Less Intimidating:** Smaller projects mean fewer pieces, fewer steps, and fewer chances for mistakes. You'll gain skills little by little, without feeling overwhelmed.

Chapter One

Getting Started with One-Yard Sewing

Before we jump into the fun projects, it's important to build a simple foundation. Knowing which fabric to choose, understanding basic sewing terms, and getting familiar with your tools will make the whole process easier and more enjoyable.

Choosing the Right Fabric for Your Project

Not all fabric is created equal, and the type you choose will affect how your project looks and feels.

- **Cotton:** The best choice for beginners. It's sturdy, easy to cut, and doesn't slip around. Perfect for tote bags, pillow covers, and table runners.

- **Linen:** Breathable with a natural texture. It wrinkles easily but works well for aprons, scarves, or home décor.
- **Fleece:** Soft and cozy, great for blankets, scarves, or kids' projects. Bonus: fleece edges don't fray, so you don't always have to finish them.
- **Canvas or Denim:** Heavier fabrics ideal for bags, storage bins, or items that need durability.
- **Knit Fabric (like jersey):** Stretchy and comfortable, used for clothing. Trickier for beginners but manageable with practice.

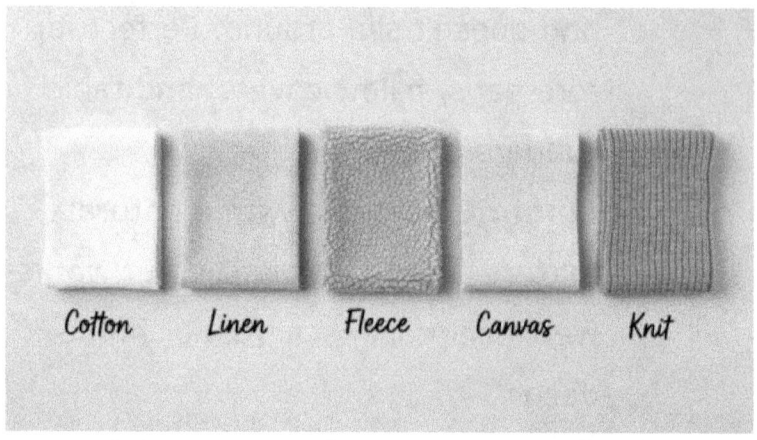

Understanding Fabric Terms

Sewing has its own "language," but once you understand the basics, patterns and instructions will make sense.

- **Selvage:** The tightly woven edge of the fabric that prevents fraying. Often has little white dots, text, or a border design.

- **Grain:** The direction of the threads in the fabric. Cutting along the grain helps projects hold their shape.
- **Bias:** The diagonal direction across the fabric. Fabric cut on the bias stretches more, which is helpful for curved projects like headbands or clothing trims.

Basic Tools Every Beginner Needs

You don't need a full sewing studio to start—just a few essentials:

- **Fabric Scissors:** Sharp scissors reserved only for cutting fabric (never paper).
- **Pins or Clips:** Hold fabric pieces together while you sew.
- **Rotary Cutter and Cutting Mat (optional):** Makes straight cuts quick and precise.

- **Measuring Tape or Ruler:** Essential for accurate measurements.
- **Iron and Ironing Board:** Pressing fabric before and after sewing gives a neat finish.
- **Sewing Machine:** A simple, beginner-friendly machine is enough. It should do straight and zigzag stitches.

Quick Guide to Sewing Stitches and Seams

Mastering a few basic stitches will open the door to most beginner projects.

- **Straight Stitch:** The most common stitch—strong and simple. Used for almost everything.
- **Zigzag Stitch:** Helps finish raw edges so they don't fray. Also adds flexibility for stretchy fabrics.
- **Finishing Edges:** You can finish raw edges with a zigzag stitch, pinking shears (scissors with a zigzag blade), or by folding the edge under and stitching it down (called hemming).

Chapter Two

One-Yard Sewing Tips and Tricks

Working with only one yard of fabric can feel limiting at first, but with the right approach, you can stretch it into multiple projects or create something that looks bigger and more polished than you'd expect. This chapter shares smart ways to cut, match, and use fabric efficiently—plus a few shortcuts and warnings to save you frustration along the way.

Maximizing Fabric Use (Layout and Cutting Tips)

The way you cut your fabric makes all the difference. Planning your layout before you make the first cut ensures you get the most out of your yard.

- Always **iron your fabric** first to remove wrinkles before measuring and cutting.
- Place your **pattern pieces close together**, aligning straight edges with the grain.
- Use a **rotary cutter and ruler** for precise cuts and less wasted fabric.
- If a project calls for smaller pieces, **map out your cuts on paper first** to avoid surprises.
- Save every leftover scrap—they're useful for trims, pockets, or small accessories.

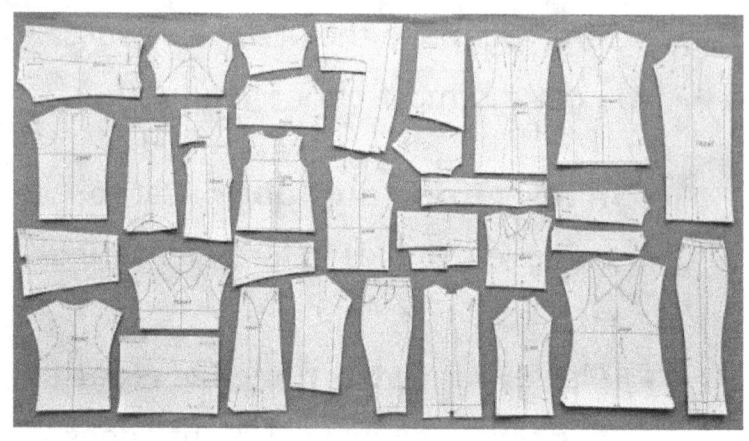

How to Mix and Match Fabric Scraps

One yard may not always be enough for a whole project, but mixing different fabrics can make your creations even more unique.

- Stick to a **color palette** (e.g., all pastels, or a mix of bold primary colors).

- Combine **patterns with solids** for balance—if you use a floral print, pair it with a plain color.
- Use small scraps for **accents** like pockets, appliqués, or decorative trims.
- Don't be afraid to experiment—scrap mixing often leads to one-of-a-kind results.

Time-Saving Hacks for Beginners

Sewing doesn't have to be time-consuming. Here are a few tricks to make your projects faster:

- **Chain sewing:** When making multiple seams, feed one piece after another without cutting the thread in between.
- **Use fabric clips instead of pins** for quicker setup.
- **Pre-wind extra bobbins** so you don't have to stop mid-project.
- **Batch cut fabric pieces** if you plan to make the same project more than once.
- **Skip pinning small straight seams**—just hold them carefully as you sew.

Common Mistakes to Avoid When Working with Small Yardage

Learning to sew with one yard is all about efficiency. Here are a few beginner mistakes to watch out for:

- **Cutting without a plan:** Wasting fabric on the first cut leaves you short for the rest of the project.
- **Ignoring the grain:** Cutting against the grain can make projects twist or lose shape.

- **Over sewing:** Too many stitches can weaken fabric or make seams bulky.
- **Forgetting seam allowances:** A half-inch off can ruin a one-yard project, so measure carefully.
- **Using the wrong fabric weight:** Heavy fabrics for light projects (like scarves) or flimsy fabrics for heavy-duty items (like bags) won't hold up.

Chapter Three

Home Décor Projects (One Yard)

Project 1 — Easy Throw Pillow Covers

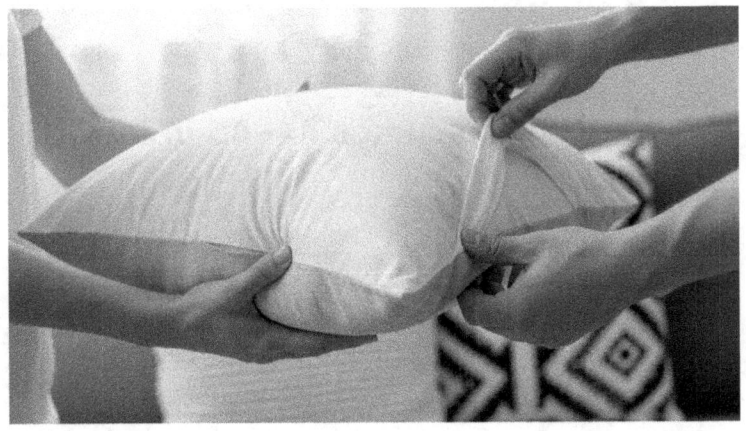

Two simple ways to use one yard to make an 18 x 18 inch (finished) pillow cover: a quick two-piece cover, and an envelope-back cover that needs no zipper.

Materials

Cutting (assumes 44–45 in fabric width)

- For both methods use a 1/2 inch seam allowance. Metric: 1/2 in = 1.27 cm.
- Simple two-piece cover: cut two squares 19 in x 19 in (48.3 x 48.3 cm).
- Envelope-back cover: cut one square 19 in x 19 in for the front,

plus two rectangles 19 in x 13 in (48.3 x 33 cm) for the back overlap.

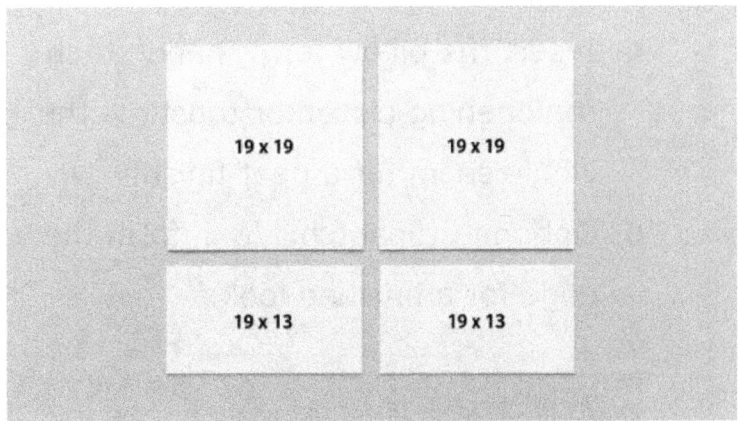

Method A — Simple two-piece cover

1. Place the two 19 x 19 in squares right sides together. Pin around edges.
2. Sew all the way around using a 1/2 in seam allowance, leaving a 3 inch opening on one side for turning.

3. Clip the corners diagonally to reduce bulk. Turn right side out, press edges flat.
4. Insert the pillow form, hand-stitch the opening closed or topstitch the whole seam for a neat finish.
5. Optional: topstitch 1/8 in from the edge for a finished look.

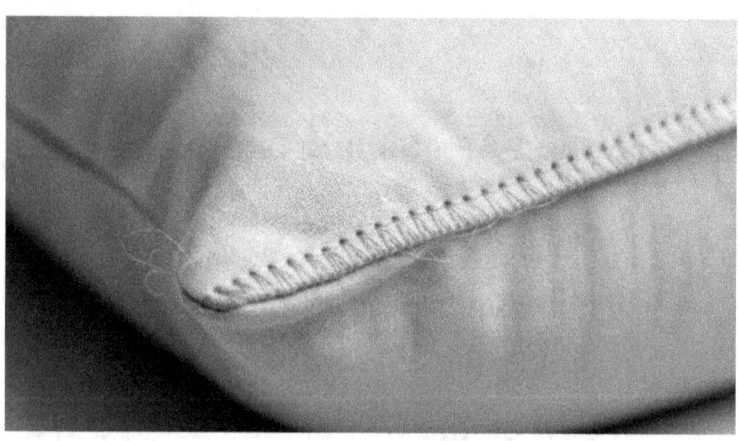

Method B — Envelope-back cover (no zipper)

1. Hem one long edge of each 19 x 13 in rectangle by folding 1/4 in, then 1/2 in, and stitching. These hems will be the exposed overlap edges.
2. Place the front square right side up. Lay one back rectangle right side down along the left edge, overlapping the middle. Lay the second back rectangle right side down along the right edge so the two rectangles overlap by about 4 in in the center. Align edges and pin.
3. Sew around the perimeter with a 1/2 in seam allowance. Clip corners, turn right side out, press.
4. Insert pillow and enjoy.

Project 2 — Reversible Table Runner

A simple reversible runner sized roughly 14 in x 43 in finished. This layout uses the width of standard fabric to get a longer runner.

Materials

- 1 yard fabric (44–45 in wide), or one yard plus scraps for contrast
- Matching thread, iron, pins, rotary cutter or scissors

- Optional: quilting batting for a quilted look

Cutting

- Finished runner: about 14 in wide by 43 in long (35.6 x 109.2 cm). Add 1/2 in seam allowance all around.
- Cut two rectangles: 15 in x 44 in each (38.1 x 111.8 cm). One is the top, one is the backing.

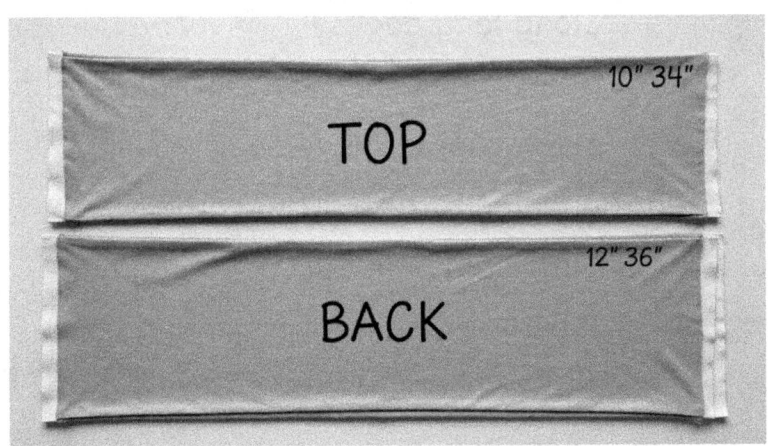

Steps

1. If using batting, cut a batting piece 14 in x 43 in. Baste top fabric, batting, and backing together.
2. If you want a quilted look, mark lines and quilt now using your machine, or skip quilting for a flat runner.
3. With right sides together, align top and backing rectangles. Pin or clip along long edges.
4. Sew around the runner with a 1/2 in seam allowance, leaving a 3 in opening to turn. Trim corners.
5. Turn right side out, press, and topstitch 1/8 in from the edge to close the opening and secure the edges.
6. Press well and lay on the table.

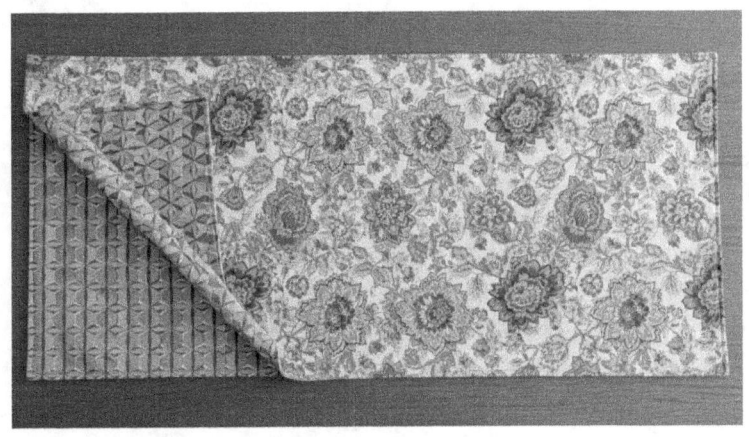

If fabric width is narrow

- You can rotate the pattern so length comes from fabric width. I recommend testing layout on paper first so you don't run short.

Project 3 — Fabric Storage Bins (small, boxed-corner style)

A structured small bin, great for drawers or shelves. Finished size here is about 7 in square base, 6 in tall. This pattern fits well into one yard with lining and light interfacing.

Materials

- 1 yard fabric (outer)
- Matching thread, iron, pins
- Medium-weight interfacing, either iron-on or sew-in (same amount as fabric)

- Optional: stiff base insert (cardboard or thin plastic) cut to base size

Cutting

- Outer fabric: one rectangle 20 in x 14 in (50.8 x 35.6 cm)
- Lining fabric: one rectangle 20 in x 14 in
- Interfacing: one rectangle 20 in x 14 in
- You will box the corners to create the base. These sizes include seam allowances.

Steps

1. Fuse or sew interfacing to the wrong side of the outer fabric panel following manufacturer instructions.
2. With right sides together, fold the outer fabric rectangle lengthwise

and sew the short side seam to form a tube. Press seam open. Repeat with the lining, leaving a 3 in gap in the lining seam for turning.

3. Box the corners for both outer and lining: measure and mark a square from each corner equal to the base size, 7 in across the corner, then fold so the seam lines align, and sew across the marked line. Trim off the triangle, leaving 1/4 in seam allowance. Do this for all four corners.

4. Turn the outer piece right side out. Keep the lining wrong side out. Insert the outer piece into the lining so right sides are together. Align top raw edges and sew all the way around.

5. Pull the bin right side out through the hole left in the lining. Hand-stitch or machine-stitch the lining opening closed. Push lining down into the bin and press the top edge. Topstitch near the top for a neat finish.
6. Insert an optional stiff base for structure.

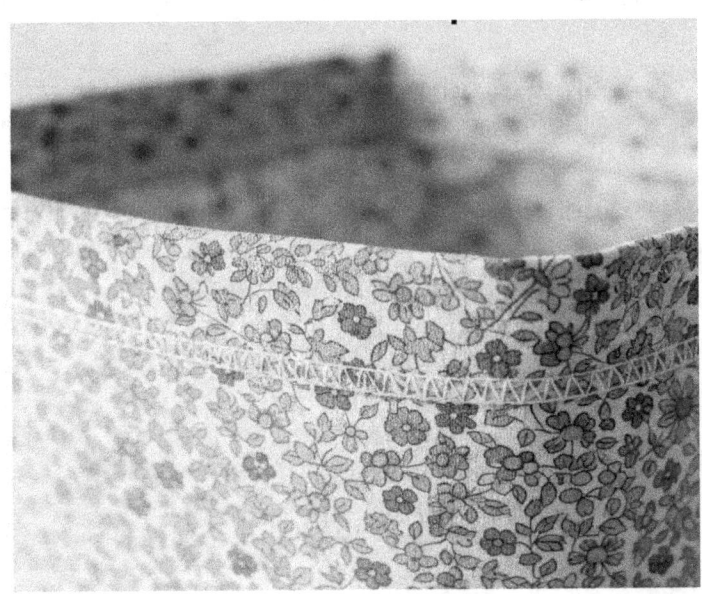

Project 4 — Curtains or Café Valances

A simple rod-pocket café valance that suits a small window, or a short curtain panel. Finished valance about 36 in wide by 16 in tall.

Materials

- 1 yard fabric, rod or tension rod, matching thread, iron, pins

Cutting

- Cut one rectangle 36 in x 18 in (91.4 x 45.7 cm) including seam allowances. If your fabric width is 44 in, you can place the long 36 in side along the length or across the width depending on window shape.

Steps

1. Hem the two short edges: fold 1/4 in, then 1/2 in, press and stitch.
2. Fold the top edge down enough for your rod plus seam allowance. For example, fold down 1 in plus 1/2 in seam, so a 1.5 in rod pocket. Press and stitch close to the fold. Leave a clean hem at the bottom with a 1/2 in seam turned twice.
3. Hang on the rod and adjust gathers to fit the window width. If you want more fullness, use the same valance

plus simple trimmed fabric or a decorative trim.

Project 5 — Fabric Coasters and Placemats

Make a set of 4 coasters and 2 placemats from a single yard. Coasters are quick gifts, and placemats are practical.

Materials

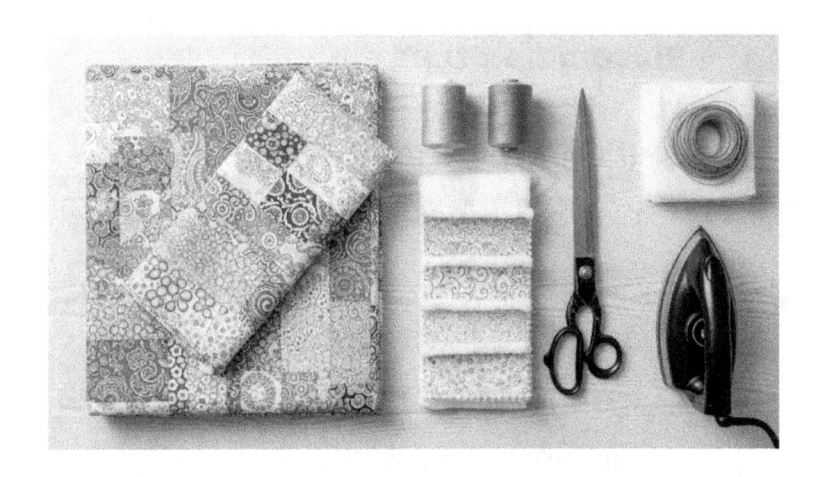

Cutting

- Placemats: cut two rectangles 13 in x 17 in each (33 x 43 cm), these give a finished mat near 12 x 16 in after a 1/2 in seam allowance.
- Coasters: cut eight squares 5 in x 5 in each (12.7 x 12.7 cm) for coasters. You can use leftover fabric or cut from the same yard.

Placemats Steps

1. If using batting, cut two batting pieces 12 in x 16 in. Layer top fabric, batting, and backing, baste, and quilt as desired. If not using batting, place right sides together for top and backing.
2. Sew around with 1/2 in seam allowance leaving a 3 in opening. Turn, press, and topstitch 1/8 in from the edge.
3. Repeat for the second placemat.

Coasters Steps

1. Place two 5 in squares right sides together. Sew around leaving a 1 in opening. Clip corners, turn, press. Topstitch close to the edge. For extra thickness, sandwich a small

square of batting inside before sewing.

Chapter Four

Fashion & Accessories Projects

Notes before you start

Seam allowance: 1/2 inch (1.27 cm) unless noted.

Fabric: 1 yard = 36 in (91.44 cm). Standard fabric width used here is 44–45 in (111.8–114.3 cm). Measure first and adjust if your yard is narrower. Press as you go for a neat finish.

Project 1 — Tote Bag and Reversible Shopping Bag

Simple, roomy tote you can make quickly. Reversible option uses the same steps with an extra lining piece so there is no exposed seam.

Materials

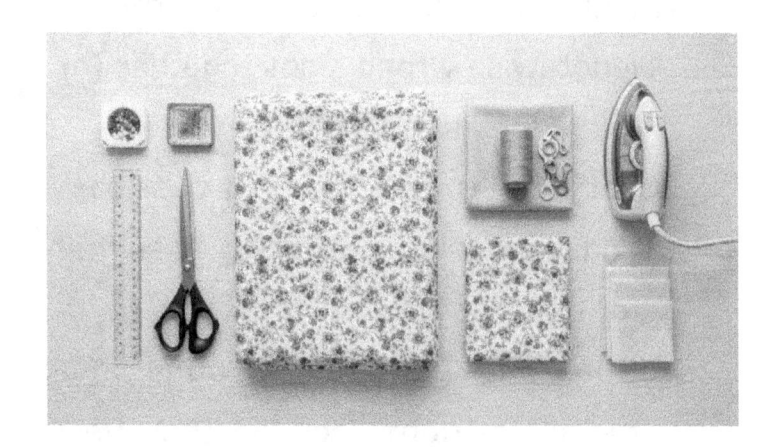

Cutting

- Outer: two rectangles 16 in x 18 in (40.64 x 45.72 cm)
- Lining (for reversible): two rectangles 16 in x 18 in (40.64 x 45.72 cm)
- Handles: two strips 4 in x 28 in (10.16 x 71.12 cm). If you prefer shorter handles, cut to 22–24 in (55.88–60.96 cm).

Steps

1. Finish straps: fold each 4 in strip lengthwise wrong sides together (or fold edges to center then fold in half), press, and topstitch close to edges. If using interfacing, fuse first for extra strength.
2. Outer bag: place the two outer rectangles right sides together. Sew

each side and bottom with 1/2 in seam allowance, leaving top open. Press seams. Repeat for lining but leave a 3 in opening in bottom seam for turning if making a lined, non-reversible tote.

3. Optional boxed corners: flatten each bottom corner, measure 1.5 in from point (or desired base depth) and draw a line across, stitch, trim triangle for a boxed base.

4. Turn outer bag right side out. If reversible: insert outer bag into lining bag so right sides face, align top edges and pin. Insert straps between layers at the points you want them to sit (about 4 in from side seam). Sew around top with 1/2 in seam allowance, turn through lining opening, or if reversible,

simply turn right side out and topstitch the top edge about 1/8 in to secure and close any turning gap.

5. Topstitch around the top edge for a finished look and extra strength.

Project 2 — Simple Skirt (Elastic Waist)

A. Simple Elastic Waist Skirt (one-yard version)

This is a relaxed gathered skirt that works well for children and for many adults when you measure first. Important: measure hips and waist before cutting.

Materials

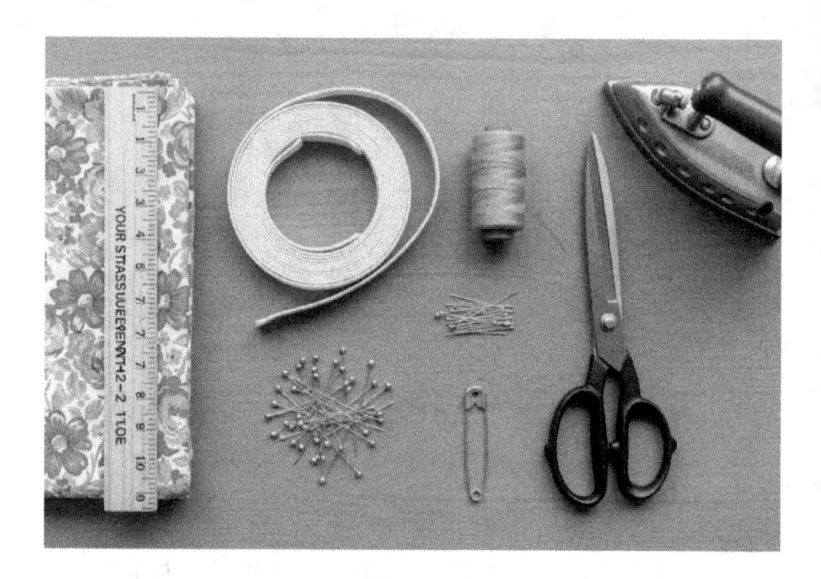

Cutting

- Cut one rectangle: full fabric width (about 44 in / 111.8 cm) by desired finished skirt length plus 1.5 in (3.8 cm) for hem and casing. Example: for a 20 in (50.8 cm) finished skirt, cut 22 in x full width (55.88 x 111.8 cm). If you want a longer skirt and your length needed exceeds 36 in (91.4 cm) you will need extra fabric.

Steps

1. Hem the bottom: fold up 1/4 in, then 1/2 in, press and stitch around.
2. With right sides together, sew the short ends of the rectangle to make a tube (1/2 in seam). Press seam open. You now have the skirt tube.
3. Create the casing for elastic: at the top edge fold down 1 in (for a 1 in elastic) plus 1/4 in seam allowance, press and stitch about 1/8 in from the raw edge leaving a 2 in opening to insert elastic. Make sure the channel is wide enough for the elastic to slide through.
4. Attach a safety pin to the elastic and thread through the casing, making

sure not to lose the other end. Overlap elastic ends by 1 in and sew securely with a bar tack or zigzag stitch. Distribute gathers evenly. Close the casing opening by stitching.

5. Give a final press.

B. Easy Apron (full bib or half waist)

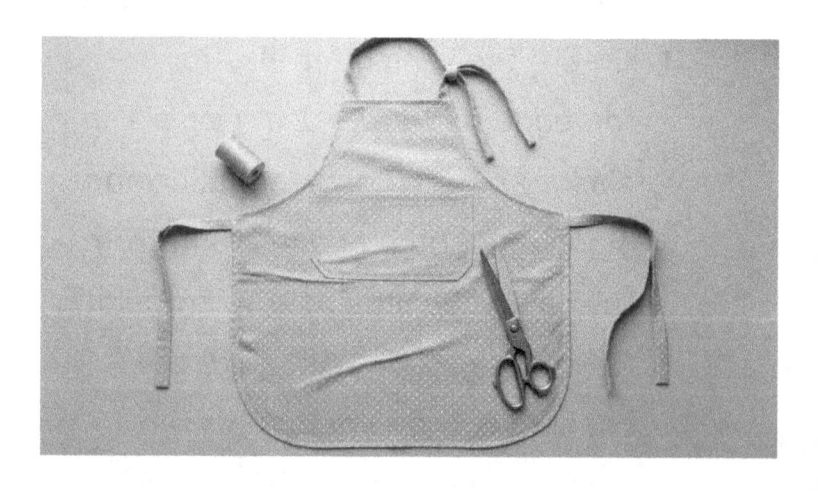

A full apron uses minimal fabric and is a classic one-yard project.

Materials

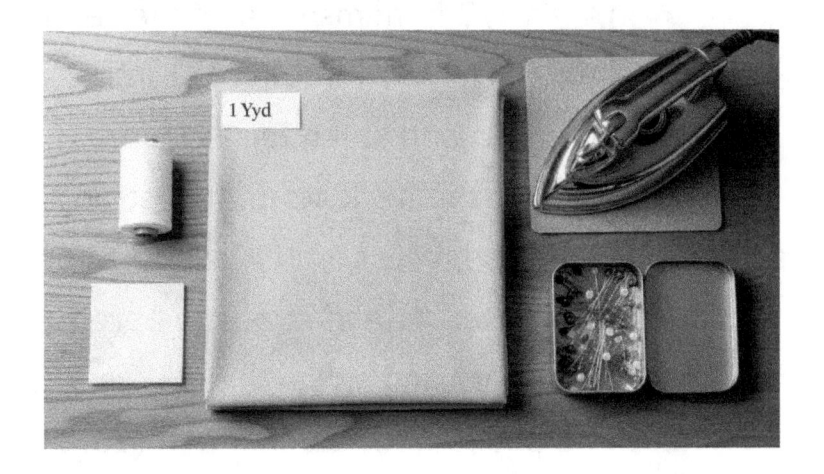

Cutting

- Full bib apron: cut one rectangle 20 in x 30 in (50.8 x 76.2 cm) for body, two strap pieces 4 in x 28 in (10.16 x 71.12 cm) for ties/neck strap. If you prefer a half apron, cut 18 in x 24 in (45.72 x 60.96 cm).

Steps

1. If making a bib, fold and press 1/4 in then 1/2 in hems on all edges and stitch, or fold 1/4 in then 1/2 in on raw edges and stitch for a clean hem. For the neck strap, fold strap lengthwise, press, stitch and turn for a tidy strap. Attach straps to apron top corners and sides.
2. For a pocket: cut a 6 in x 8 in (15.24 x 20.32 cm) scrap, hem top edge, fold under sides, topstitch to the apron body centered or offset as desired.
3. Press and topstitch around the edge of apron for a finished look.

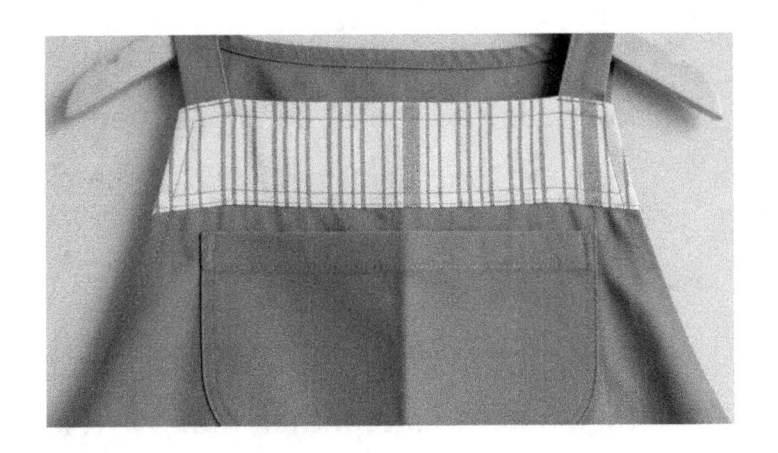

Project 3 — Infinity Scarf

Option A: Quick Single-Loop Infinity Scarf (fast)

Steps

1. Fold right sides together along the long edge so the 12 in edges meet. Sew the long edge with 1/2 in seam allowance to form a tube.
2. Turn tube right side out and press. Fold tube in half widthwise and sew the short ends together with a 1/2 in seam, creating a loop. Tuck seam flat and topstitch if desired.

Concept

Cut two or three long strips from your yard along the length and sew them end-to-end for a longer band you can loop twice.

Steps

1. Sew the short ends of strips together to create one long tube. Press seams flat. Fold right sides together lengthwise, stitch long edge to make a tube, turn right side out, then sew short ends to make a loop. Tuck seam and topstitch. Twist once for a knotted effect if you like.

Project 4 — Headbands and Hair Scrunchies

Scrunchie (super quick, makes several from one yard)

Steps

1. Fold long edges toward center, then fold in half to enclose raw edges, or make a tube by folding right sides together and sewing with 1/2 in seam. Turn tube right side out and press.
2. Thread elastic through tube with safety pin, overlap elastic ends and stitch securely. Sew the fabric ends together with a small ladder stitch or

topstitch to hide the seam. Fluff the gathers.

Time: 10–20 minutes per scrunchie, yields 4–6 scrunchies from one yard depending on strip width.

Headband (classic wide or twisted)

Materials

- For a standard headband: cut 8 in x 22 in (20.32 x 55.88 cm); for twisted, cut two strips 4 in x 22 in (10.16 x 55.88 cm)
- Thread, pins, iron

Steps

1. Classic: make a tube by sewing long edge right sides together, turn right side out, press. Fold the tube in half lengthwise and stitch ends together

to form a loop, then topstitch if desired. Add a small piece of elastic in the back for comfort if you like by inserting 2–3 in elastic into a small gap.

2. Twisted: take two strips, sew short ends to make two loops, turn right side out, place loops on top of each other and twist once, then sew edges together or hand-sew a small seam at back to secure.

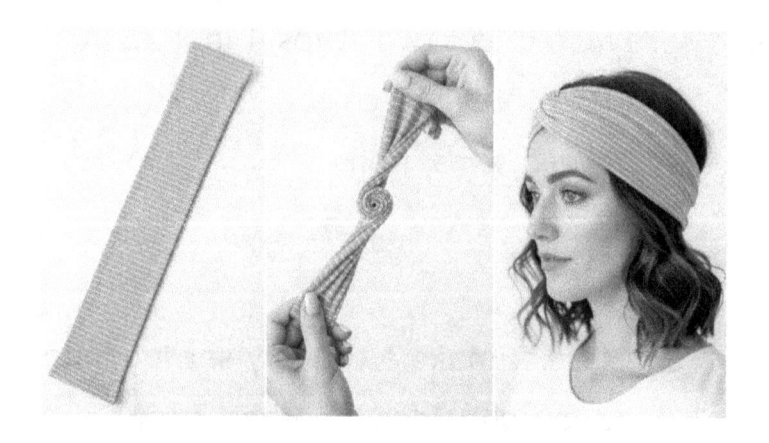

Project 5 — Fabric Belts or Sashes

Make a simple tie sash or a narrow belt from one yard.

Cutting

- Sash: cut one rectangle 10 in x full width (10 in x 44 in, 25.4 x 111.8 cm) for a wide sash. For a narrower belt, cut 4 in x 44 in (10.16 x 111.8 cm).

Steps

1. To make tapered ends: mark a 2 in taper at each end and cut wedges so ends come to soft points. Fold the long edges to center then fold again and stitch down the length for a clean, reversible sash. Alternatively, sew long edges right sides together leaving a small gap, turn right side out, press, and topstitch.
2. For a belt with a buckle, insert interfacing for strength and create a narrow finished tube to thread through the buckle. If you need more length, sew two strips end-to-end and disguise the seam with a decorative wrap or knot.

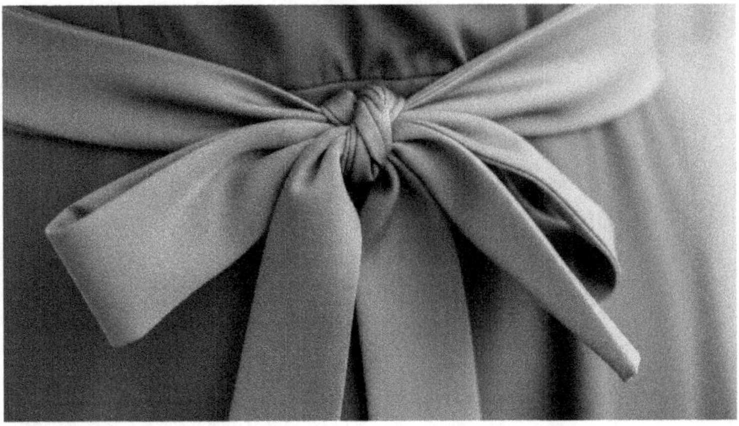

Chapter Five

Gift & Personal Projects

Quick note before you start
Always pre-wash and press your fabric if it is washable. That prevents shrinkage and gives a neater finish. Seam allowance throughout is 1/2 inch (1.27 cm) unless I say otherwise.

Project 1 — Reusable Gift Bags (Drawstring and Flat-Handled)

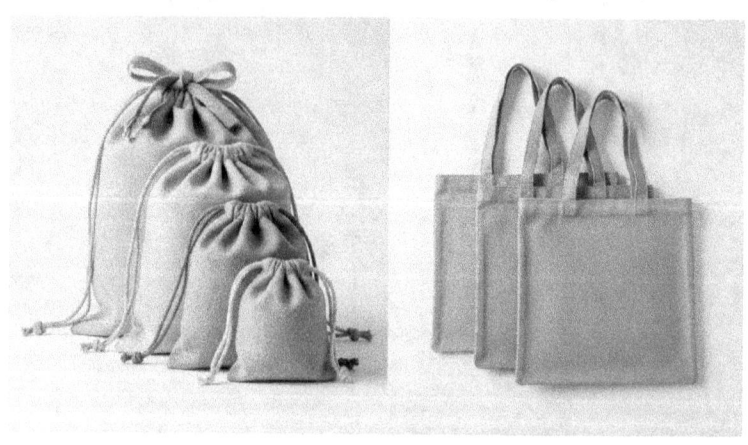

Two simple styles you can make from one yard: a drawstring gift bag and a flat-handled gift bag.

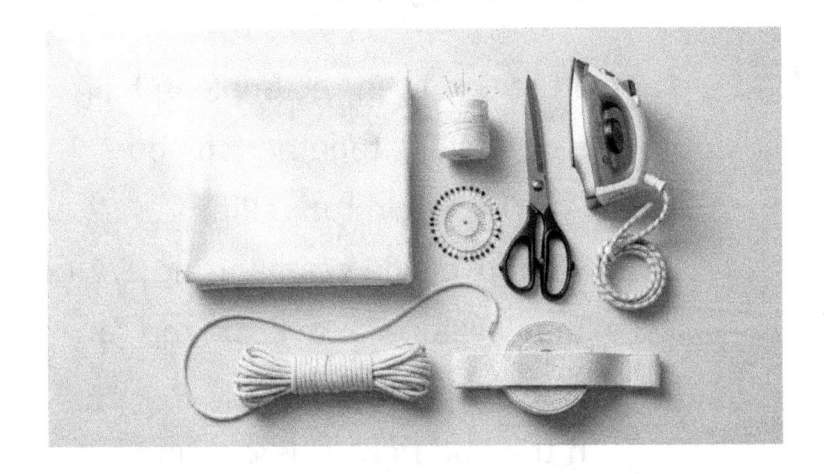

Cutting (finished sizes shown)

- Drawstring bag (finished about 8 x 10 in): cut one rectangle 9 x 11 in (22.9 x 27.9 cm).
- Flat-handled bag (finished about 8 x 10 in): cut one rectangle 18 x 11 in (45.7 x 27.9 cm) for the body (this

will be folded), plus two handle strips 2.5 x 22 in (6.4 x 55.9 cm).

Drawstring Bag Steps

1. Fold the 9 x 11 in rectangle in half with right sides together so you have a 9 x 5.5 in tube. Pin.
2. Sew the two side seams using 1/2 in seam allowance. Leave the top raw edge open.
3. Turn the bag right side out and press. On the top edge, fold down 1/4 in, press, then fold down 1 in (this creates the casing). Stitch close to the lower fold but leave a 1.5 in opening to thread your cord.
4. Thread cord or ribbon through the casing using a safety pin, tie the ends, and pull to close. Trim any long tails.

5. Optional: topstitch 1/8 in from the top for a neat finish.

Flat-Handled Bag Steps

1. Fold the 18 x 11 in rectangle in half widthwise with right sides together to make an 9 x 11 in tube. Sew the two side seams with 1/2 in allowance. Press seams open.
2. Finish the top edge by folding 1/4 in, then 1/2 in and stitching.
3. Prepare handles: fold each 2.5 x 22 in strip lengthwise, press, then open and fold long edges to center and fold again. Stitch close to both long edges.
4. Pin handles to the inside of the bag on the right side at positions about 2 in from each side seam. The handle

ends should be tucked under the hem.

5. Turn bag right side out and topstitch around the top to secure handles. Optionally box the bottom corners for depth by measuring 1.5 in from each corner, drawing a line, and sewing across. Trim corners.

Project 2 — Wine Bottle Bag

A smart way to present a bottle. Add a padded lining if you want a more luxurious feel.

Cutting

- Outer fabric: one rectangle 13 x 17 in (33 x 43 cm).
- Lining: one rectangle 13 x 17 in (same size).
- Optional base: cut a small square of cardboard or interfacing about 4 x 4 in (10 x 10 cm) to insert into boxed base.

Steps

1. If using batting, fuse it to the wrong side of the outer fabric. Press.

2. Place outer pieces right sides together and sew the long side and one short side, forming a tube with one short side open. Repeat for lining but leave a 3 in gap in the short side seam for turning.
3. Box the bottom: open the closed bottom corner so the side seam and bottom seam align, measure 2 in from the point and draw a line perpendicular to the seam. Sew across that line. Trim the triangle leaving 1/4 in seam allowance. Do this for all four corners if you want a square base, or just for two opposite corners to create a flatter base.
4. Turn the outer bag right side out. Insert outer bag into the lining (right sides together). Align the top raw

edges and pin. Sew all the way around the top edge.

5. Pull bag through the gap in the lining so the bag turns right side out. Hand-stitch or machine-stitch the lining gap closed, tuck lining inside, press, and topstitch close to the top edge for a clean finish.

6. Optional: add a ribbon tie around the neck or sew a small loop and button closure.

Project 3 — Travel Pouch / Zipper Bag (Lined)

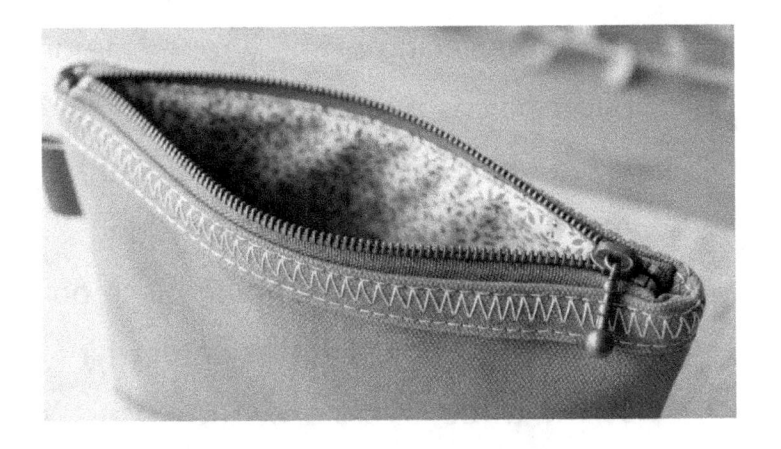

A lined pouch with a zipper. Make it in one of the common sizes for travel kits.

Cutting (finished pouch about 8 x 5 in)

- Outer: two rectangles 9 x 6 in (22.9 x 15.2 cm)
- Lining: two rectangles 9 x 6 in
- Optional interfacing: two rectangles 9 x 6 in

Steps

1. Fuse interfacing to the wrong side of outer pieces if using. Press.
2. Place one outer piece right side up. Align zipper right side down along the top edge. Place a lining piece on top of the zipper (right side down) so the three layers are stacked: outer right side up, zipper face down on outer, lining face down on zipper. Pin and sew using a zipper foot. Repeat with the other outer and lining pieces on the opposite side of the zipper.
3. Open the zipper halfway. Press the fabric away from the zipper teeth so it lies flat, then topstitch along the zipper for a neat finish.
4. With right sides together, sew around the three open sides of the pouch with a 1/2 in seam allowance,

leaving a 2-3 in gap in the lining for turning. Clip corners.

5. Turn the pouch right side out through the gap and push lining into the pouch. Close the gap in the lining with a ladder stitch or topstitch close to the edge if you prefer.

6. Give a final press.

Project 4 — Fabric Book Cover / Journal Cover

A neat wrap-style cover that protects a paperback or hardback and adds a personal touch

Cutting (for a standard paperback about 8 x 5 in)

- Main piece: cut one rectangle 12 x 10 in (30.5 x 25.4 cm). This gives enough material to fold into corner pockets. For larger books adjust length by book height + 4 in and width by book width x 2 plus 1 in.

Steps

1. Optional: press interfacing to the wrong side of your main fabric for stability.

2. Fold the short edges in toward the center about 1/2 in and press. Then fold each short edge again about 2 in to form the pocket flap that will hold the book cover. Press and stitch close to the inner fold to create the pocket.
3. Place the book on the center of the fabric and slip the front cover into one pocket and the back cover into the other so the fabric wraps around the book snugly. If you like, add an elastic band or ribbon closure by sewing a small loop to the back cover that wraps around the front.
4. For a removable insert style, make two inner corner pockets by folding small squares into each interior corner and topstitching to secure.

That will hold the book corners firmly.

Project 5 — Sleep Mask and Eye Pillow

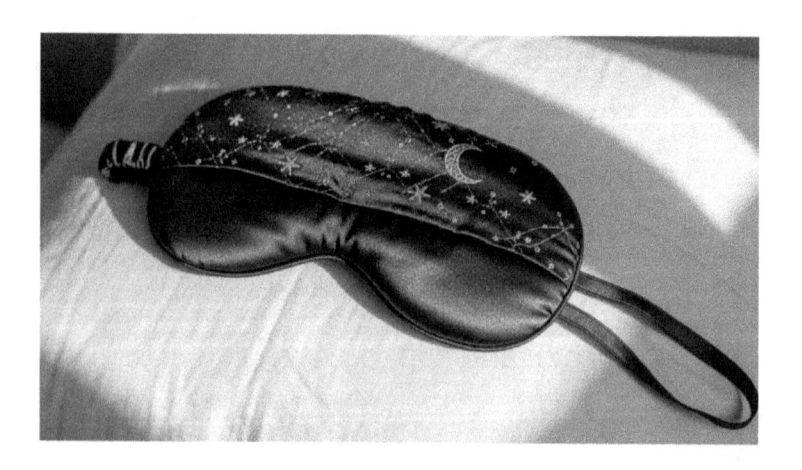

Two comfy bedside projects. A sleep mask is lightweight and washable. An eye pillow can be filled with flaxseed and dried lavender for a calming scent and optional microwave warming.

Cutting

- Sleep mask: one outer piece 9 x 4.5 in (22.9 x 11.4 cm), one lining 9 x 4.5 in, elastic 12–14 in (30–36 cm) depending on comfort.
- Eye pillow: outer cover two rectangles 9 x 4.5 in for a slip cover and inner bag two rectangles 7 x 3 in for the filler pouch.

Sleep Mask Steps

1. Draw a gentle mask shape on paper to use as a template. Cut two fabric pieces using the template.

2. Place right sides together and sew around, leaving a 2 in gap for turning. Clip curves.
3. Turn right side out, press, and insert elastic ends into the side seams before closing the gap (or attach elastic on the outside then topstitch the seam). Hand-stitch or machine-stitch the gap closed and topstitch around the edge to flatten and secure.
4. Optional: add a thin layer of batting between the layers for extra cushioning.

Eye Pillow Steps

1. Sew the inner bag: place the 7 x 3 in pieces right sides together and sew three sides leaving one short side open. Turn right side out. Fill

with about 1/2 to 3/4 cup of flaxseed or rice and a teaspoon of dried lavender if using. Do not overfill; leave room to flatten. Sew the opening closed with a small seam.

2. Make an outer cover from the 9 x 4.5 in pieces right sides together. Sew around leaving an opening, turn right side out, press, then insert the filled inner bag. Close the outer cover opening with a ladder stitch or topstitch.

3. If you want a microwaveable eye pillow, make sure both fabric and filler are microwave-safe and heat in 15–20 second intervals only.

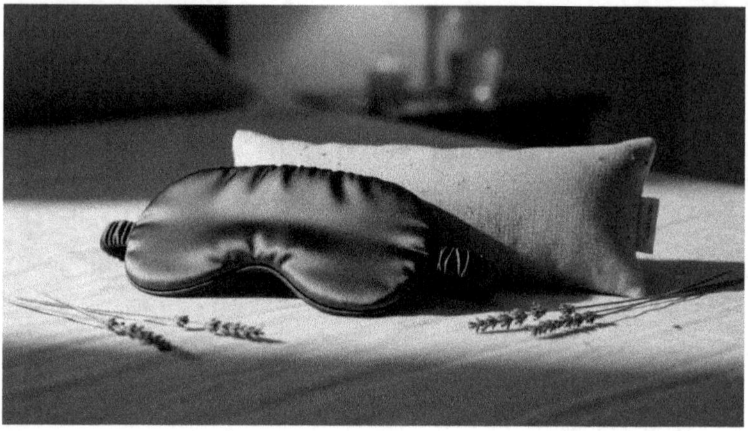

Chapter Six

Kids & Fun Projects

Quick note before you start: pre-wash and press fabric when appropriate. Seam allowance used throughout is 1/2 inch (1.27 cm) unless noted. Measurements assume a standard fabric width of 44–45 inches (112–114 cm). For any project intended for children under 3 years old, avoid small parts like buttons or beads; use embroidery or securely sewn felt pieces instead.

Project 1 - Simple Doll Clothes or Doll Blanket

Two quick, satisfying options: easy doll clothes for an 18-inch doll (adjustable) and a small doll blanket.

Materials

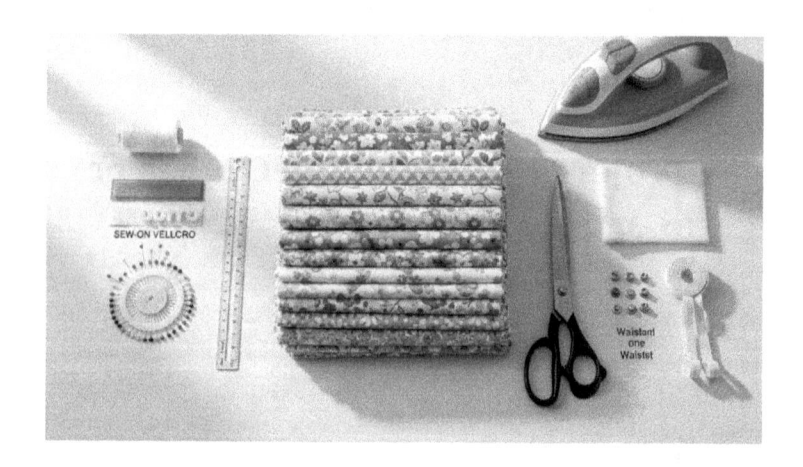

Doll T-shirt (easy)

Cutting (18-inch doll)

- Front/back: two rectangles 6 in x 8 in (15.2 x 20.3 cm)
- Sleeves: two rectangles 3 in x 4 in (7.6 x 10.2 cm)

Steps

1. Fold each sleeve piece in half widthwise, press and sew the short edge to create a sleeve tube.
2. Place front and back pieces right sides together. At the top edge, leave a 2 in gap in the center for the neck opening. Sew side seams from bottom up to where sleeves will attach, leaving arm openings.

3. Pin sleeves to the arm openings, matching raw edges and easing if needed. Sew sleeves in place.
4. Finish neck by folding the top edge inward 1/4 in, then another 1/4 in, and topstitch, or add a small strip of bias tape.
5. Turn right side out and press. Add Velcro at the back neck if the neck needs to open.

Simple Elastic Skirt for Doll

Cutting

- One rectangle 8 in x 6 in (20.3 x 15.2 cm)

Steps

1. Hem the bottom: fold 1/4 in, then 1/2 in, press and stitch.

2. Sew the short ends right sides together to form a tube. Press seam.

3. Fold the top down to create an elastic casing about 1/2 in wider than your elastic. Leave a 1 in opening, thread elastic with a safety pin, sew elastic ends together, and close the casing. Even out gathers.

Doll Blanket

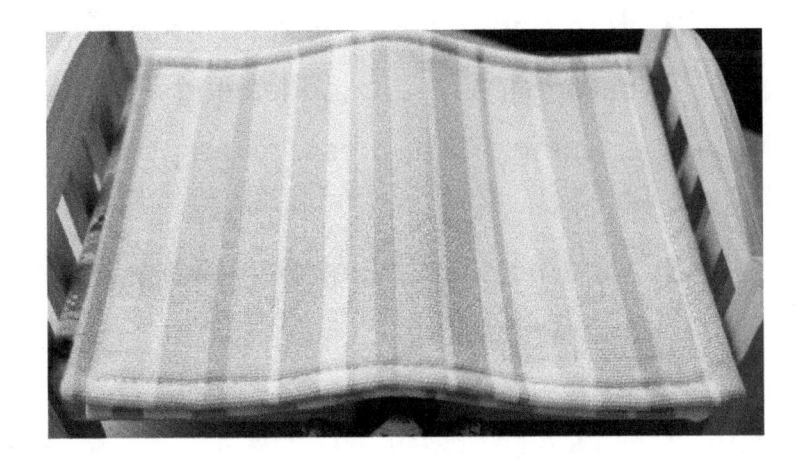

Cutting

- One rectangle 14 in x 18 in (35.6 x 45.7 cm). Add batting if you want a padded blanket.

Steps

1. Layer top fabric, batting, and backing (if using). Baste and quilt simple straight lines or leave flat.
2. With right sides together (if no batting), sew around leaving a 3 in opening. Turn, press, and topstitch to close.
3. For a finished edge, bind with a 1/2 in bias binding.

Project 2 - Drawstring Bag for Toys

A handy toy bag, great for stuffed animals or building blocks.

Cutting

- One rectangle 15 in x 18 in (38.1 x 45.7 cm) for a roomy bag

Steps

1. With right sides together, fold rectangle in half so it becomes 15 in x 9 in. Sew side seams with 1/2 in seam allowance.
2. Hem the top twice: fold 1/4 in, then 1 in to create a casing for the drawstring, leaving a 1.5 in gap for threading. Sew around.
3. Turn right side out, press. Thread cord through casing using a safety pin. Knot the ends, or add wooden beads if safe for the child's age.
4. Optional: box the bottom corners for more depth by flattening each corner and sewing across 1.5 in

from the point, then trimming the triangle.

Project 3 - Fabric Crown or Headband

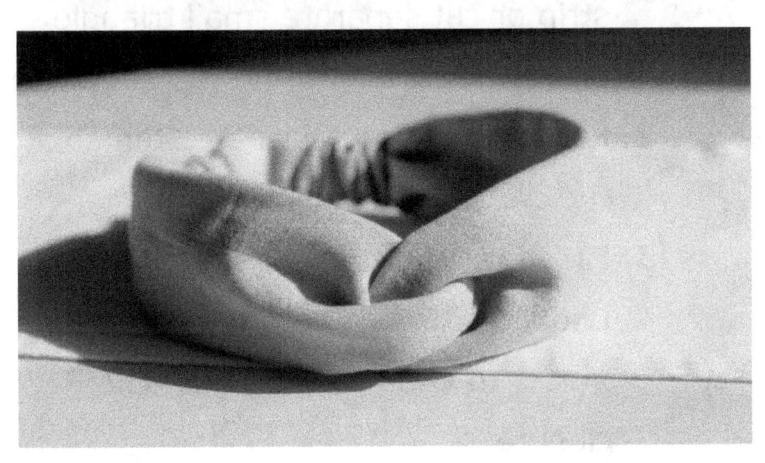

Perfect for dress-up and parties. Crown is simple and adjustable with Velcro.

Cutting

- Crown strip: cut a strip 4 in high x 22 in long for toddler size (4 in x 56 cm). Adjust length for older children.
- Add triangles or scallops for the crown top, about 3 in tall (7.6 cm).

Steps - Crown

1. Draw and cut crown points from the strip or cut separate small triangle pieces and stitch to the top edge.
2. Fuse interfacing if using cotton so the crown holds shape.
3. Finish raw bottom edge by folding under 1/4 in and topstitching. Attach Velcro to ends for an adjustable closure.

4. Decorate with felt shapes, pom-poms, or fabric glue-on gems. For safety, sew embellishments rather than glue for items that will be handled a lot.

Steps - Headband

1. For a soft headband, follow the same tube method used earlier: cut 4 in x 22 in, sew tube, turn, press, stitch ends together, and add optional elastic at the back for stretch.

2. For a structured headband, cover a plastic headband with fabric strips and glue or stitch.

Project 4 - Mini Soft Toys or Stuffed Animals

Start with a simple heart, star, or bunny shape before trying more complex patterns.

Cutting (example - heart toy)

- Two heart shapes about 6 in tall x 6 in wide (15.2 x 15.2 cm)

Steps

1. Place two shapes right sides together. Sew around leaving a 2 in opening. Clip curves and corners as needed.
2. Turn right side out, push out shapes with a blunt tool, stuff firmly but not overly tight.
3. Hand-sew the opening closed with an invisible stitch. Add embroidered face details or securely stitched felt features.
4. For a bunny, add separate ear pieces, stitch them, and attach before stuffing.

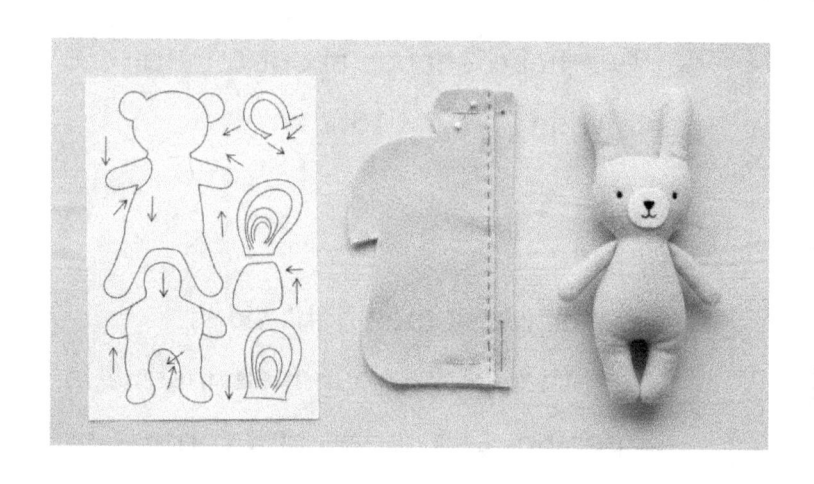

Project 5 - Kid's Apron

Sized for kids, with a simple neck loop and waist ties. Make in two sizes:

toddler (2-4 years) and child (5-8 years).

Cutting

- Toddler size: 16 in x 18 in body (40.6 x 45.7 cm)
- Child size: 18 in x 22 in body (45.7 x 55.9 cm)
- Straps: two 2 in x 24 in strips for ties, one 2 in x 10 in for neck loop (folded)

Steps

1. Hem all edges by folding 1/4 in then 1/2 in and stitching.
2. Attach neck loop: fold and press neck strap, secure to top corners, or make a loop with Velcro for adjustable neck size.

3. Attach waist ties at the side seams, or sew them into the side seams before finishing the edges.
4. Add a pocket: cut a 6 in x 6 in square (15.2 x 15.2 cm), hem the top edge, fold sides under and topstitch to the apron body. Reinforce pocket corners with a short diagonal stitch.

Chapter Seven

Seasonal & Holiday Projects

Quick note before you start
Pre-wash and press washable fabrics to prevent shrinkage and to get clean cuts. Seam allowance throughout is 1/2 inch (1.27 cm) unless I say otherwise. Where I give example sizes, treat them as starting points and adjust to fit your taste or the actual object you are making.

Project 1 — Christmas Stockings (classic cuffed stocking)

Materials

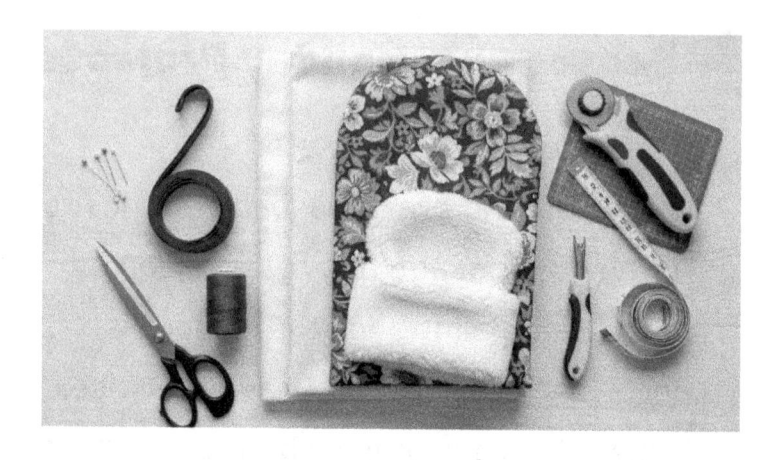

Finished sizes (examples)

- Adult stocking, about 18 inches long by 9–10 inches wide at the widest point (18 in = 45.72 cm, 10 in = 25.40 cm).
- Child stocking, about 14 inches long by 7–8 inches wide (14 in = 35.56 cm).

Cutting

1. Make a paper template, draw the stocking shape at the finished size you want, then add 1/2 inch seam allowance around the template. (Picture idea: photo of a paper template traced onto fabric.)
2. Cut two outer pieces, two lining pieces, and a cuff strip: 4 in high by the stocking width plus seam allowance (for an 18 in stocking, cuff about 4 in x 10 in finished, cut 4.5 in x 11 in to include seam allowance and folding).

Steps

1. With right sides together, sew the two outer stocking pieces along the edge using 1/2 inch seam allowance, leaving the top open. Clip curves and trim seam allowance at curves

to reduce bulk. Repeat for lining pieces, but leave a 3 inch gap in one side seam of the lining for turning.

2. Turn the outer stocking right side out and press. Insert the outer stocking into the lining so right sides face, aligning tops. Sew around the top edge to join the outer and lining together.

3. Pull the stocking through the turning gap in the lining so the outer fabric is right side out and the lining is inside. Hand-stitch the turning gap closed or topstitch close to the top edge.

4. Create the cuff by folding the cuff strip in half lengthwise, press, and align raw edges to the stocking top, then stitch around. Fold cuff down to cover the seam.

5. Attach a small fabric loop at the stocking top seam for hanging, secure with bar tacks or several back-and-forth stitches. Add appliqué, embroidery, or name tag as desired.

Project 2 — Halloween Trick-or-Treat Bag (simple fold-and-sew tote, optional lining)

Finished size (example)

- About 12 inches wide by 14 inches tall (12 in = 30.48 cm, 14 in = 35.56 cm).

Cutting

1. Cut one rectangle 24 in x 14 in (61.0 cm x 35.6 cm). You will fold this piece in half widthwise to form the bag body. If you want a boxed bottom, plan for boxed corners later. (Picture idea: flat rectangle with marked center fold.)

Steps

1. Fold the 24 x 14 in rectangle in half so it becomes 12 x 14 in, right sides together. Sew the two side seams with 1/2 inch seam allowance. If you want a boxed bottom, open the bottom corner and measure across to make a 2 in to 3 in square, stitch across, trim the triangle, then turn and press.
2. Finish the top edge by folding 1/4 inch and then 1/2 inch, press and stitch. If you want a drawstring closure, fold the top down enough to make a casing for the cord, stitch leaving a small opening to thread

the cord. Thread the cord using a safety pin and knot the ends.

3. If you prefer handles, cut two strips for handles, fold and stitch as in previous chapters, and attach them securely to the top edge before topstitching. Add spooky applique, felt pumpkin, or stitched ghosts for decoration.

Boxed-corner

Project 3 — Valentine's Day Heart Pillow (decorative throw pillow)

Finished size (example)

- Heart about 10 inches tall across the longest dimension (10 in = 25.40 cm).

Cutting

1. Draw a heart template on paper at the finished size, then add 1/2 inch seam allowance around the shape. Cut two outer pieces from main fabric. (Picture idea: drawn heart

template and two heart-shaped fabric pieces ready to sew.)

Steps

1. Place heart pieces right sides together. Pin, then sew around with 1/2 inch seam allowance leaving a 2 to 3 inch opening at the bottom or side for turning. Clip curves carefully to allow the heart to turn smoothly.
2. Turn the heart right side out and gently push out the curves with a blunt tool. Press lightly, then stuff with polyfill to the desired fullness. Do not overstuff.
3. Hand-stitch the opening closed using an invisible stitch, or topstitch around the edge close to the seam for a finished look. Add a little ribbon loop at the top if you want to

hang it. Optionally add embroidery or an appliqué heart for extra layering.

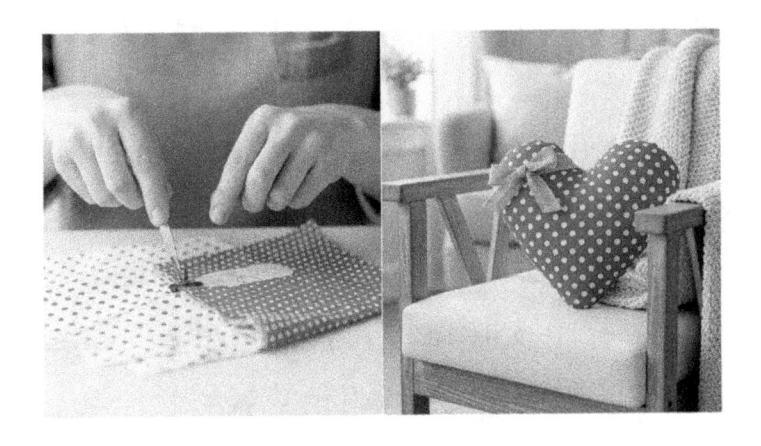

Project 4 — Easter Basket Liner (round or boxed bottom)

This fits most small store-bought baskets. Use a removable liner so it can be washed.

Measure first

1. Measure your basket base diameter and depth. For a small basket example, base diameter 8 inches, depth 6 inches. If you have a different basket, use those measurements.

Cutting (example for 8 in base, 6 in depth)

1. Trace the basket base onto paper or fabric to get an exact circle, then add 1/2 inch seam allowance around the traced line and cut the base circle. (Example base 8 in = 20.32

cm, cut with 1/2 in added around edge.)

2. For the side panel, cut a rectangle equal to the basket circumference plus 1/2 inch seam allowance, by desired depth plus seam allowance. To estimate circumference, multiply base diameter by pi, for an 8 in base circumference is about 25.13 inches, so cut a side rectangle about 25.5 to 26 in long by 7 in high to include seam allowances and a little ease. (Picture idea: traced circle and side rectangle laid out, ruler showing measurements.)

Steps

1. Sew the short ends of the side rectangle together with 1/2 inch

seam allowance to form a tube. Press seam open.

2. Pin the side tube right sides together to the base circle, aligning raw edges. Ease the side fabric as you go and stitch all around, using 1/2 inch seam allowance. Trim seam allowances and notch if needed for a smooth curve.

3. Finish the top edge by folding 1/4 inch then 1/2 inch and stitching to make a neat hem, or create a casing for elastic or drawstring by folding down a wider hem and stitching, leaving a small opening to thread elastic or ribbon. Insert elastic and secure, or thread ribbon for ties.

4. If you want a ruffled trim, sew a 2 in to 3 in strip gathered and attach to the top edge before finishing the

hem. Make the liner removable by leaving the top edge flush or adding a tie to secure it to the basket.

Project 5 — Summer Picnic Placemat or Picnic Tote

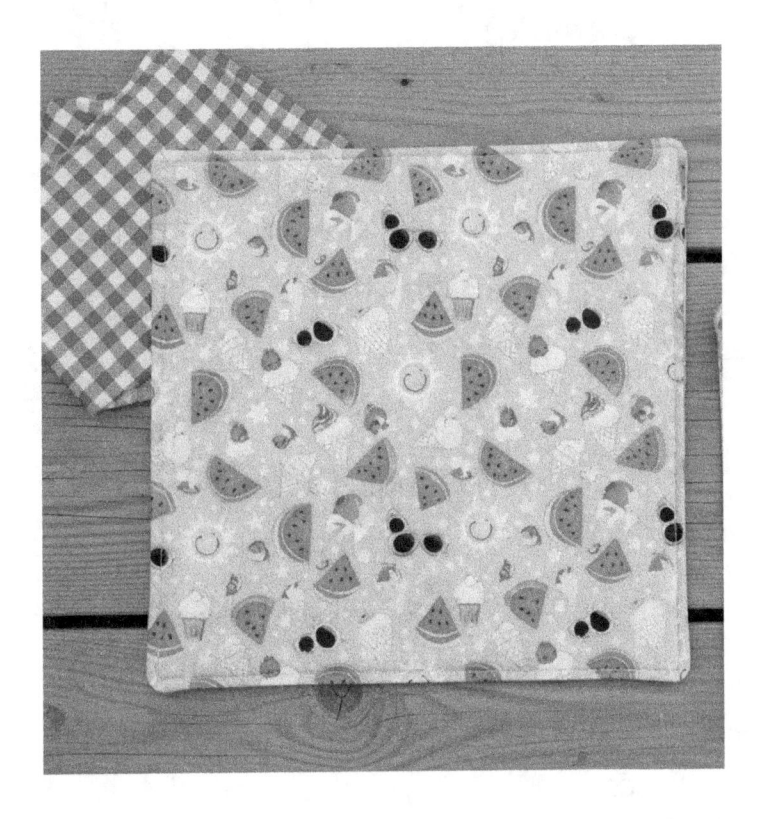

Two sunny options you can make from one yard. Choose the placemat for quick gifts, or the tote for a reusable picnic carrier.

A. Picnic Placemat (quilted, reversible)

Finished size

- 12 in x 18 in finished placemat (12 in = 30.48 cm, 18 in = 45.72 cm).

Cutting

- Cut two rectangles 13 in x 19 in each, that accounts for 1/2 inch seam allowance all around, plus optional batting pieces 12 in x 18 in. (Cut size 13 x 19 in = 33.02 x 48.26 cm.)

Steps

1. Layer top fabric, batting if using, and backing fabric, baste, and quilt as desired (straight lines are quickest). (Picture idea: quilt sandwich pinned and a quilting step.)
2. With right sides together, sew around leaving a 3 inch opening, clip corners, turn right side out, press, and topstitch close to the edge to close the opening and secure the outer edge. Repeat for a set. Add a fabric napkin pocket on one side if you like.

B. Picnic Tote (simple insulated or non-insulated carry bag)

Finished size (example)

- About 12 in square base by 16 in tall (base 12 in = 30.48 cm, height 16 in = 40.64 cm).

Cutting

- Cut two rectangles 24 in x 17 in, fold in half to make two panels 12 in x 17 in, these become the outer and the lining. Add batting or insulating foam cut to 12 x 16 in for structure. (24 in x 17 in = 61.0 x 43.18 cm.)

Steps

1. Fuse or quilt the batting between outer and lining panels if insulating, or skip batting for a lightweight tote.
2. With right sides together, sew side seams and bottom seam for outer panel. Repeat for lining but leave a 3 inch gap in the lining bottom for turning. Box the corners by flattening and stitching across 2 in from the points to create a flat base. (Picture idea: boxed corner diagram

and a tote with open top showing interior.)

3. Turn outer bag right side out, insert into lining (right sides together), align top raw edges and sew, leaving an opening if you prefer a reversible tote. Turn through the lining gap or pull outer through if making non-reversible, then close the lining gap and topstitch the top edge.
4. Make handles from 4 in x 22–28 in strips, reinforce them with extra stitching, and place them about 3 to 4 in from the side seams. Add an interior pocket for napkins or cutlery if desired.

Chapter Eight

Beyond One Yard

Seam allowance throughout is 1/2 inch (1.27 cm) unless noted. In this chapter you will learn how to scale up by combining one-yard projects into larger pieces, how to use leftover scraps so nothing goes to waste, and practical ways to personalize projects with embroidery, trims, buttons, and more. Photo notes are included where a picture will really help the reader.

Combining multiple one-yard projects into bigger creations

Working one yard at a time is great, but you can also join finished pieces or partial pieces to make larger, coordinated items. Below are three simple, repeatable ideas with step-by-step instructions.

1) Make a coordinated home set: runner + placemats + coasters

Materials

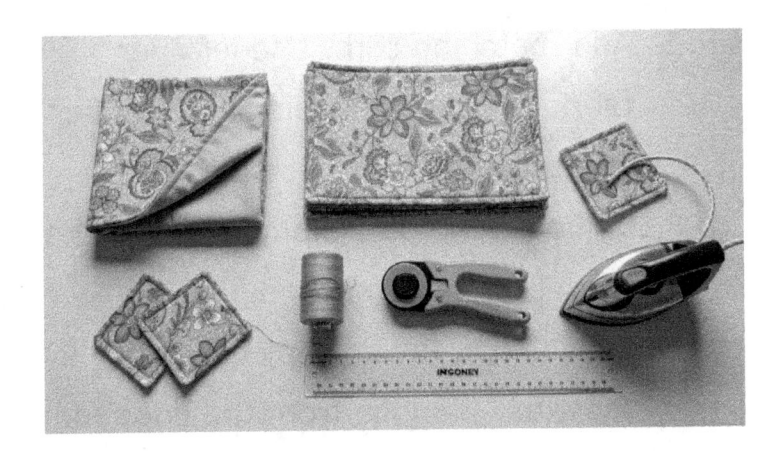

Steps

1. Plan. Lay out all finished pieces on a table to see how patterns line up and where repeating motifs should sit. (Picture idea: overhead layout showing runner, placemats, coasters arranged together.)

2. Match edges. If a motif on the runner should align with a placemat, trim the placemat backing slightly so the pattern is centered. Mark placement with pins.

3. Add matching trim. Use leftover fabric to make bias binding or piping and topstitch it to each piece for a unified look. (See piping steps in the embellishments section.)

4. Final finish. Press all pieces and topstitch 1/8 inch from the edge for a consistent, shop-made finish.

2) Patchwork throw or lap quilt from small projects and scraps

Steps

1. Cut into uniform blocks. Trim existing finished panels to the same block size (for example 5 to 6 inch squares, unfinished). (Picture idea: pile of trimmed squares in neat columns.)

2. Sew blocks into rows. Join squares into strips right sides together, pressing seams to one side. Join strips to make the quilt top.

3. Layer sandwich. Make a quilt sandwich: quilt top, batting, backing. Baste.
4. Quilt and bind. Quilt by straight-line stitching or free-motion if you prefer. Finish with binding made from leftover fabric.

3) Bigger bags and organizers from multiple projects

Example: Turn a tote plus small zipper pouch and coasters into a gift set.

Steps

1. Reserve one yard for the tote. Use another yard or scraps for the pouch and coasters.
2. If straps need reinforcement, stitch scrap pieces to the strap underside or fuse interfacing to scraps and wrap around straps. (Picture idea: tote with matching pouch clipped to the handle.)
3. For a more structured organizer, sew small pocket panels from scraps and stitch them inside the tote before attaching the lining.

How to use fabric scraps left over from projects

Start by sorting scraps so they are easy to find. Keep three bins or boxes: large pieces (12 inches and up), medium pieces (6 to 12 inches), and small bits (under 6 inches). Below are practical scrap projects and step-by-step instructions.

A. Strip piecing and strip quilts

Good for medium-width scraps.

Steps

1. Cut strips 2 to 3 inches wide from scrap pieces. Straighten edges with a ruler and rotary cutter.

2. Sew strips end-to-end with diagonal seams to reduce bulk, pressing seams open.
3. Cut joined strip sets into blocks and assemble into a quilt top or table runner.

B. Continuous binding from scraps

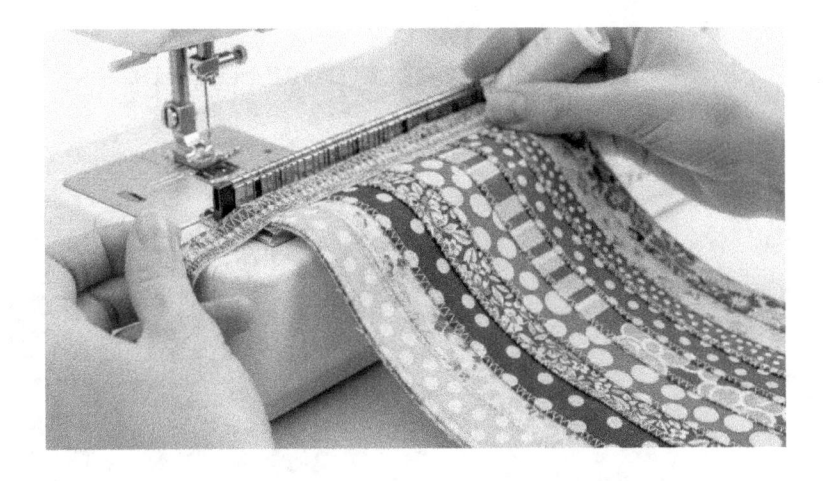

Turn uneven leftovers into neat binding.

Steps

1. Cut 2.5 inch strips, join them on the bias or straight grain using 45 degree seam joins for a smooth continuous length.

2. Press seams open, fold and press in half lengthwise, then attach to your project following standard binding technique.

C. Coasters, patch pockets, and appliqué

Small squares make great coasters or pockets.

Steps - Coaster

1. Cut two 5 x 5 inch squares and one 5 x 5 inch batting square.
2. Layer right sides together with batting on the outside, sew leaving a small opening, clip corners, turn, press, topstitch.

Steps - Appliqué pocket

1. Cut a pocket shape from medium scrap, finish raw edge or use fusible web, baste in place, then topstitch.

D. Fabric flowers, yo-yos, and trims

Great for tiny scraps.

Steps - Yo-yo

1. Cut a circle about 3 to 4 inches diameter.
2. Run a running stitch around the edge, gather, and knot to form a yo-yo. Attach to headbands, crowns, or gift bags.

E. Small accessories from tiny bits

- Scrunchies, key fobs, zipper pulls, and brooches are perfect for tiny leftovers.
- Use interfacing or small inner seams to add strength where needed.

Tips for personalizing: embellishments, embroidery, buttons, trims

Personalization makes projects feel handcrafted and unique. Test everything on a scrap first.

Embroidery basics

Tools: embroidery hoop, embroidery needle, stranded cotton, small scissors, water-soluble transfer pen or iron-on transfer paper, tear-away stabilizer for knits.

Steps - Simple motif (a single flower or initial)

1. Transfer design to fabric using tracing or a transfer pen. (Picture idea: design in hoop ready to stitch.)
2. Hoop fabric with stabilizer underneath. Use backstitch for outlines, satin stitch for filled areas, and French knots for tiny dots.
3. Finish the back with a small piece of tear-away stabilizer or trim threads neatly.

Tip: Use shorter stitch lengths on

lightweight fabrics to avoid puckering.

Appliqué and raw-edge appliqué

Two common methods:

- Fusible raw-edge appliqué: fuse shapes with fusible web, then edge-stitch with a narrow zigzag.
- Turned-edge appliqué: use a template, turn edges under, and hand- or machine-sew in place.

Steps - Fusible appliqué

1. Trace shape on fusible web, fuse to fabric scrap, cut out.
2. Peel backing, position on project, press to adhere. Stitch around the edge with narrow zigzag or straight

topstitch.

Buttons, snaps, and closures

Placement and reinforcement matter. Steps - Sewing on a button

1. Mark button placement, use a small patch of interfacing behind lightweight fabric.
2. Sew through holes several times for strength. If the button will be handled frequently, use a shank or create a small thread shank for ease of use.

3. For snaps or magnetic closures, follow manufacturer instructions and reinforce with interfacing.

Adding trims and piping

Trims instantly upgrade a basic item.
Steps - Inserting piping

1. Make piping by encasing cord in a narrow strip of fabric and stitching close to the cord.
2. Insert piping into the seam allowance when sewing two panels together, then stitch the seam to

catch the piping.

Labels, tags, and finishing details

- Sew in a small woven label at a side seam or add a fabric tag for a maker's mark.
- Press and grade seams at curves. Clip curves for smooth turns and press each seam for a polished finish.

Conclusion

Sewing with just one yard of fabric may seem limiting at first, but as you've seen throughout this book, it opens the door to endless creativity. From simple home décor pieces to fashion accessories, gifts, and even seasonal projects, one yard is enough to make something practical, beautiful, and personal.

The best part is that these projects are approachable, even for beginners. They're budget-friendly, quick to complete, and a great way to build sewing confidence without the stress of handling large amounts of fabric. As you grow more comfortable, you can start combining projects, using scraps, and adding your own embellishments to make every creation truly your own.

Remember, sewing is as much about the process as it is about the finished item. Every cut, every stitch, and every small project helps you build skills that will carry into bigger creations. Most importantly, it gives you the joy of making something with your own hands.

So gather your fabric, set up your tools, and let your imagination guide you. With just one yard, you now have everything you need to begin a lifelong journey of creativity and handmade beauty.